I0476805

Change Management Guide: Empowered Management of Business Change

Brian Kail, MBA, CPC, CCC

Cover image by Denis Ismagilov/123rf.com
Cover designed by One18 Design

ISBN: 1523351276
ISBN-13: 9781523351275
Library of Congress Control Number 2016904193

DEDICATION

Dedicated to my wife, and partner Royce. I could not have completed this work without her support, and love. Thanks also to my four footed friends for the many ways they enrich my life.

CONTENTS

ACKNOWLEDGMENTS

I want to acknowledge the help and support I have received from many in the business community, and those in the coaching, and speaking industries. This includes public figure, and speaker Joe Schmit, business development expert Marc LeBlanc, social media consultants Theresa, and Dick Fisher, author, and speaker Michael Thomas Sunnarborg, executive coach Jim Carr, and the Minneapolis-St. Paul MetroNorth Chamber of Commerce. Avery special thanks to fellow coaches, Monica J. Smith, and Bina Patel. Thanks to all for your help, encouragement and guidance.

Prologue

Man considering the universe sees nothing but changes in matter, forces, and mental states. He sees that nothing really is, but that everything is becoming, and changing.

Source, *"The Kybalion Hermetic Philosophy"*

Chapter 1
Why Managing Change Matters

Change is a given. From a personal perspective, I have made at least four career changes. I went from marketing support to sales to computer consultant to network manager to business analyst and finally to career coach/public speaker. Each move was a world of change. So a career change is a significant change, and there is a niche of coaches for job-transition issues. But in addition to career change, where do other changes come from in the business world?

One source of change is a morphing economic environment. Our economy is a world economy, and changes in Asian economies—such as growth, sales, import, export, and buying trends—very much impact our US economy. On a national level, in addition to the above factors, interest rates and political shifts impact the US economy. Most US companies need to be aware of this changing economy and business environment to survive. Changes in the external environment often drive changes within companies. These changes within an organization may manifest themselves in changes in products, niche markets, manufacturing, processes, and sometimes methodology.

Because my calling is to improve business quality of life (BQL), I am most interested in those changes within business that impact the individual directly. In addition to a career change or loss of job, the common changes that impact the professional directly are the following:

1) Changes in management
2) Changes in job duties
3) Changes in how the work is to be done
4) Change due to acquisition/merger
5) Change in company policy.

Based on my thirty-plus year experience in corporate life, I believe the single most common source of change is new management, and that change often drives other changes as listed above. On a personal note, I worked for a large financial institution, and there was a change in my supervisor every six to twelve months.

So often I have seen professionals and management respond to change in a way that projects that they are powerless to change. The most important message I want to send out is that you *do* have power when impacted by change. You have power that no one can take away. You are in a very real way empowered but don't see it. As with many things in life, the first, most important aspect of dealing with an issue is to recognize it. Have you been informed of a change in management? A change in job duties or responsibility? A change in *how* you are to do your job? Or a change in the product of your job? If you answered yes to any of these, you need to recognize you have been impacted by change. In future segments we will look at what options we have in change and that engagement is the best response to change. But for now, realize you are only a victim of change if you perceive yourself as such. Rejoice! You are *empowered!*

Looking Ahead: Below are the nine steps that make up empowered change management:

1) Hear the change
2) Ask questions
3) Measure the impact
4) Decide
5) Follow through

6) Implement

7) Track the change

8) Report the success

9) Celebrate the change

CHANGE MANAGEMENT GUIDE

BRIAN KAIL, MBA

Chapter 2
Step One: Hear the Change

Executive Summary: The first step toward best management of change is to actively hear the message of change. Actively listen with the assumption that the change is important and will impact your life. Plan on taking notes.

Background Story:

I remember on more than one occasion while I was in high school, a teacher presented our class with a special test. We were all told to take our seats, be quiet, and pay attention, as we would be taking an important test on communication and following instructions. Once we were settled and had our number-two pencils, the teacher gave us instructions. The most important was to read the entire test before beginning. The two-page test was handed out to all in the class. The test was a mix of vocabulary, science, and math questions. Many were very difficult. We were told to begin the test. Most of us feverishly dug into the test, concerned only with the question we were currently working on. There were difficult questions, like "One train is leaving Lisbon at fifty miles per hour headed for Vienna; a second train is leaving Paris, also headed for Vienna, at fifty-five miles per hour. Which train will reach Vienna first, and will they pass each other?" Some of us asked for scratch paper and tried to run equations. Still others, the socially adept, looked around the classroom to others for some hint of what was going on, and to see whether there was any way to complete the test on time. Usually, out of a class of thirty or so, one or two students would stand up and hand the test back to the teacher after about ten minutes or so. Could one or two students be that much smarter than the rest of us? The key was hidden in plain sight, at the very bottom of the test sheet. It read, "This has been a test in listening. Do not record any answers to questions, but return this test back to the instructor." This was a painful lesson in how not to listen. We were even told twice, "Read the entire test before recording any answer." Even though the instructions said to read the ENTIRE test before recording answers, our first mistake was in failing to listen to the message. Most of us failed to actively *hear* the initial message and failed the test.

Step One: Hear the Change

This piece is so important that it needs to be called out as a distinct step. I also want to make a distinction between "listening" and "hearing." To me, listening is passive. There may or may not be something worth hearing. To best address change, assume that the change you are hearing about is important and will impact your life. To help focus on the message, take the perspective, "How will this change I am about to hear impact my business quality of life?" This will give the active act of listening more urgency. When you are about to hear of a change in your business, or in your life in general for that matter, the most important message on change is to understand that you are not passive in the change. Said another way, my most important message to you when you are facing change is that you do not have to be passive. The first *active* step is to hear the message of change with the assumption that the message is important and will impact you. Your active task is give your full attention to the information about the change and actively process the information to arrive at the message of what the change really is and what its impact will be upon you and others.

Below is a list to consider when presented with a change. Actively hearing the message of change is the first step in negotiating change:

- Have you set aside enough time to hear the message?
- Can you be free of distractions to hear the message?
- How will you handle "chatter" around you that may distract from the message?
- Do you have a way to take notes?
- Do you need to let others know you are unavailable so you can hear the message?
- Will you be able to explain the change in simple terms to a colleague after hearing it?
- Could you describe the change in one page or less if you were asked to?
- In simple terms, can you explain the reason(s) that led to the change?
- How might the change impact your business, your department, and your customers?

In summary, be prepared to actively hear the message of change. Have the right amount of time, the right tools, and the right frame of mind. To best address change, you need to actively hear the message of change from the perspective that there is an important message here. It is your job to decipher what the change is.

Looking Ahead: Actively hearing the change is the foundation for the steps to come. In the next chapter, we will introduce the second step in the nine-step system. Step two is to ask questions. The challenge will be to ask the right questions. Listening actively and critically is the foundation for step two—asking questions.

Progress: We are at step one, Hear the change.

The nine steps of empowered change management:

1) Hear the change: Make the assumption that the message of change you hear will be important and will impact you.

2) Ask questions: If you do not fully understand the change or its potential impact, it is your job to ask questions. But make sure they are the right questions.

3) Measure the impact: What are the benefits of the change? When will they be realized? What is the measure of success for the change?

4) Decide: Decide whether you will support the change as stated or negotiate the terms of the change. This is the most empowering step of the nine!

5) Follow through: Do the follow-through(s) that are needed based on your decision.

6) Implement: Own and act on your responsibilities to implement the change. Understand how problems will be escalated during implementation.

7) Track the change: Ensure that the change is being tracked. Identify the metrics and see that they are being captured.

8) Report the success: Ensure that the right teams and decision makers are fed the correct metrics around the now-implemented change. Report any peripheral or unexpected successes to the right teams. Get sign-off that the change was successful based on agreed-upon metrics.

9) Celebrate the change: Allow the organization to enjoy the success brought about by the change. This can be a morale-

building opportunity. Even if the change was not entirely successful, as long as you have engaged actively in the process, you can still find reasons to celebrate.

HEAR THE CHANGE—WORK SHEET:

PREPARATION ITEM	CHECK ITEM
Did you set aside enough time to hear the message?	
Will you be free of distractions to hear the message?	
What is your plan for handling "chatter" around you that may distract from the message?	
How do you plan to take notes?	
Have you told others you will not be available during this time?	
After hearing the message of change, could you explain the change to a colleague in simple terms?	

Will you be able you describe the change in one page or less if you were asked to?	
Capture the three most important points of the change.	
1)	
2)	
3)	
What reason(s) led to the proposed change?	
1)	
2)	
3)	
4)	

Consider how the change may impact your business, your department, and our customers. List the impacts.

1)

2)

3)

4)

5)

6)

7)

8)

9)

Notes:

BRIAN KAIL, MBA

Chapter 3

Step Two: Ask Questions

Executive Summary: To confirm that you understand the message of change, be prepared to ask questions. As a professional, it is your job to ask the right questions. Asking questions will deepen your understanding of the change.

Background Story:

Al Pacino is one of the most successful and respected actors of our time. Early films that made Al a dramatic force include *The Godfather* saga, *Dog Day Afternoon*, *Serpico*, and *Scarface*. In a documentary interview ("I Knew It Was You"), Al was asked where he learned his acting trade. Even though Al studied at the Actors Studio, Al has said that most of what he learned about acting came from John Cazale. Al had worked with John in the *Godfather* series and *Dog Day Afternoon*. Sadly, John Cazale died of lung cancer in 1978, at the young age of forty-two. But in John's short yet stellar film career, he starred in three of the most important films of the latter half of the twentieth century. Besides the three *Godfather* films and *Dog Day Afternoon*, John also starred in *The Deer Hunter*. When Al was asked why John had such a big impact on his training, Al Pacino said, "Because he asked questions." By asking questions, John would settle the set and get other actors thinking more deeply about their characters' intentions and circumstances. Al Pacino even said that it was the process of asking questions that was most important. Even if the answer was not evident, John Cazale's process of asking questions enriched the actors' performances. Here is an important message regarding the value of asking questions. We as professionals need to make sure the questions we ask are the *right* questions.

Step Two: Ask Questions

Step Two toward empowered mastery of change is to ask questions. To back up one step, this assumes you have done a responsible job of *hearing* the message. And again, listening is passive, but *hearing* is active. And if you want to be a master of change rather than a victim, you want to be active and engaged in the process as much as possible.

A thoughtful listener will ask the *right* questions. The *right* question is one that does not waste other people's time or your own valuable time. One general guideline is to stay within topic. If you have sidebar issues not related to the change you are about to address, hold those for the right time and place. If your question is emotionally charged, weigh the pros and cons of putting the question forward. The prudent option is to not engage in emotionally charged questions. But as with much in life, there can be exceptions. One exception would be to raise a flag if you feel that what is being proposed is clearly an injustice. If you are in a leadership position, there are times you do need to make a strong stand, and this may be the case. Another valid question to ask is how this change will impact your job and responsibilities. If this has been clearly stated in the message, there is no need to ask. However, if there is some gray area, a good option is to say, "So I think I heard you say my job will be impacted by…" The most important question you should consider is, "How will this change impact our customers?" As an aid, below is a list of things to consider when deciding whether your question is the *right* question:

- Has there been a time/place designated to ask questions? (If not, you need to pursue the time/place to ask questions.)

- Will my question drive an insight around the topic?

- Will my question clarify the who, where, what, and, sometimes, why around the message of change?
- Is my question on topic?
- Will my question address a gray area?
- Is my question emotionally charged?
- Will my question result in an emotional response?
- Does my question waste my time?
- Does my question waste others' time?
- Will my question bring value to my organization?
- Has my question already been asked—perhaps using different wording?
- Will my question help bring value to our customers?

In closing, a change will be more successfully implemented if a time and place are designated to ask questions. To be a master of change, it is your job to ask the *right* questions. Asking questions is an *active* process.

Looking Ahead: Steps one and two—actively hearing the proposed change and asking the right questions, in the right forum, and of the right people—are foundational steps to support the next step in the nine-step system. Step three is to estimate the impact of the proposed change. In order to estimate the impact of the change, you need to understand the elements of the organization that will be impacted. These could be human resources, system resources, revenue, and/or expenses. By actively hearing the proposed change and asking the right questions, you will have the information that you need to do your best job of estimating the impact, both good and bad, of the change.

Progress: We are at step two, Ask Questions

Here are the nine steps of empowered change management:

1) Hear the change: Make the assumption that the message of change you hear will be important and will impact you.

2) Ask questions: If you do not fully understand the change or its potential impact, it is your job to ask questions. But make sure they are the right questions.

3) Measure the impact: What are the benefits of the change? When will they be realized? What is the measure of success for the change?

4) Decide: Decide whether you will support the change as stated or

negotiate the terms of the change. This is the most empowering step of the nine!

5) Follow through: Do the follow-through(s) that are needed based on your decision.

6) Implement: Own and act on your responsibilities to implement the change. Understand how problems will be escalated during implementation.

7) Track the change: Ensure that the change is being tracked. Identify the metrics and see that they are being captured.

8) Report the success: Ensure that the right teams and decision makers are fed the correct metrics around the now-implemented change. Report any peripheral or unexpected successes to the right teams. Get sign-off that the change was successful based on agreed-upon metrics.

9) Celebrate the change: Allow the organization to enjoy the success brought about by the change. This can be a morale-building opportunity. Even if the change was not entirely successful, as long as you have engaged actively in the process, you can still find reasons to celebrate.

ASK QUESTIONS—WORK SHEET:

What types of impact will the change have to you?
1)
2)
3)
4)
What types of impact will the change have on your department or team?
1)
2)
3)
4)

5)

What types of impact will the change have on your company or organization?
1)
2)
3)
4)
5)

What types of impact will the change have on your clients or customers?
1)
2)

3)

4)

5)

Notes:

BRIAN KAIL, MBA

BRIAN KAIL, MBA

Chapter 4

Step Three: Estimate the Impact

Executive Summary: The third step in empowered change management is to estimate the impact of change. The measurement for impact may be in terms of resource changes, changes in processes, changes in policy, changes in products, and/or services. It needs to be clear what the projected impacts will be so you can make an informed decision on supporting the change.

Background Story:

This is an election year. In fact, this year we elect someone to the highest office in the United States, and really the most powerful position in the world. We elect the next president of the United States. The campaigns in both major parties have been running their course, and now there are hints of a third-party run by a very wealthy politician. At this point in the race, with the general election just a few months away, the gloves have come off. The attacks have gotten personal, even within parties. It seems the more outlandish the attacks, the more press the candidate receives. Emotions are high. Many of us respond at the emotional level. We cheer on the candidate who hits our emotional buttons the best. These buttons can be around foreign wars (as a superpower, will the United States ever see an end to these?), jobs, national security, social issues, and even religion. We respond emotionally and raise our fists in the air as if we are watching a wrestling match (think WWF). We think, "Just wait till we get Mr./Ms. So-and-So into office. Then we'll fix *their* little red wagon!" (The proverbial "their.")

But something magical and important will happen as we get close to election day. Most rational, realistic voters will start to think about the actual impact of electing their preferred candidates. To me the big litmus test is whether our next president will be able to get things done. In short, will our next president be able to make deals? For virtually any significant program to become reality, there needs to be at least partial buy-in from the opposing party. Another important measure for the next president will be whether the candidate's economic ideas add up. Most of us will ask, "If my candidate is elected, how will it impact my paycheck and savings?" Another consideration is how loans, including mortgages, will be affected if my candidate is elected. This process I am describing is estimation of the impact for election of our next president. The same process is critical when you are presented with a change in processes, policies, roles, products, and services in your organization.

Step Three: ESTIMATE THE IMPACT

Once you have actively heard the message of change and you have asked the right questions to better understand the change, you come to the third step in empowered mastery of change. We need to estimate the impact of the change with the assumption that it will be implemented. But what are we measuring the impact against? What is our ruler or scale? The pieces that impact us personally—that impact our business quality of life (BQL), or quality of life in general—will differ based on the individual. Not all of us value the same things. For me, time spent in my home has great value. So I often consider this aspect when confronted with a change. Will I need to need to travel to other offices? How frequently? And for how long? Will I need to travel out of the state? Or travel out of the country? These are all questions that I consider when weighing out a change, an opportunity.

When measuring the impact of a proposed change, you also need to consider the impact to others. What impact will the change have on your business team? On your department? Will their work be easier, or harder? In either case, what is the upside, and are there any negatives in the proposed change? Will you need to work longer hours to support the change? If so, try to quantify the number of hours, and make a projection on what the benefit will be to the team, your boss (this is an important one to consider), the department, the organization, and, most importantly, the customer. A quick way to estimate positives and negatives is to draw a line down the middle of a sheet of paper and list positives (or gains) on the left side of the line and negatives (or losses) on the right. Often these will offset each other. For example, on the right might be, "I am being asked to learn different skills," but on the left could be, "By learning new skills I will be more valuable and marketable." Or the right could read, "I am being asked to be a lead for new hires," balanced by the left, which might say, "I will gain supervisory experience." The important thing here is to put the pluses and minuses down on paper, or an electronic device, to be able to see them and weigh them out rationally. Below is a list that we can draw from when we want to measure impact:

- What resources will shift based on the change?
- What is the primary impact of change?
- What are secondary impacts of the change?

- What are the costs of the change?
- What are the benefits of the change?
- Will the entire business team be impacted?
- What will be the delta in terms of hours? (In business "delta" refers to the change observed.)
- What will the delta be in terms of effort?
- What will the impact be to business quality of life (BQL)?
- What is the measure (benefit, loss) of the change for the customer?

Again, on the topic of change, and the power of choice, the key is to take an *active* stance when working through a change. The more active you are when working through a change, the more power you have. Reject being a victim of change. Engage the change with action.

Looking Ahead: The next step, step four in the nine-step empowered change management system, is the most difficult, but also the most empowering, of the nine steps. Step four is to decide whether to support the change as presented, negotiate terms of the change, or reject the change under any condition. By actively hearing the change (step one), asking the right questions (step two), and estimating both the costs and all projected benefits of the change (step three), you will have the critical information you need to make an educated, informed decision. If you have exercised due diligence, you will be in the best position to understand what is at stake with the change in order to make the best decision.

Progress: We are at step three, estimate the impact.

Here are the nine steps of empowered change management:

1) Hear the change: Make the assumption that the message of change you hear will be important and will impact you.

2) Ask questions: If you do not fully understand the change or its potential impact, it is your job to ask questions. But make sure they are the right questions.

3) Measure the impact: What are the benefits of the change? When will they be realized? What is the measure of success for the change?

4) Decide: Decide whether you will support the change as stated or negotiate the terms of the change. This is the most empowering step of the nine!

5) Follow through: Do the follow-through(s) that are needed based on your decision.

6) Implement: Own and act on your responsibilities to implement the change. Understand how problems will be escalated during implementation.

7) Track the change: Ensure that the change is being tracked. Identify the metrics and see that they are being captured.

8) Report the success: Ensure that the right teams and decision makers are fed the correct metrics around the now-implemented change. Report any peripheral or unexpected successes to the right teams. Get sign-off that the change was successful based on agreed-upon metrics.

9) Celebrate the change: Allow the organization to enjoy the success brought about by the change. This can be a morale-building opportunity. Even if the change was not entirely successful, as long as you have engaged actively in the process, you can still find reasons to celebrate.

ESTIMATE THE IMPACT—WORK SHEET:

1) What resources will be needed based on the change?	
2) Where will the resources come from?	
3) What types of impact will come from the change? (staff workload, contractor hours, systems processing load, increased customer support, etc.)	

4) What types of costs will increase due to the change?	
5) What is the measure of the increased costs?	
6) What types of benefits will be realized due to the change?	
7) How will the benefits be measured?	

8) What will the benefits be in terms of employee workload and hours?	
9) Will effort change due to the change?	
10) How will the change in effort be measured?	

11) How will business quality of life (BQL) be impacted due to the change?	
12) How will your customers be impacted due to the change?	
13) How will impact to customers be measured?	

Notes:

Chapter 5

Step Four: Decide

Executive Summary: Step number four of change management is to make a decision on whether we support the change as presented or negotiate the terms of the change. In extreme cases, such as a breach of ethics, we may need to voice our rejection of the change. We need to proceed cautiously if our decision is to reject the change. Decision is the most empowering of any of the steps in change management.

Background Story:

Many years ago I was lead on a team that was responsible for data backup and recovery for a large Fortune 500 company. We had recently gone through a change in middle management. (At this organization these changes seemed to happen every six months to a year. Are we having fun yet?) The upper management was emphasizing customer service (not a bad thing), and they now expected our team to be on call 24-7. The good news is that this would rotate, so no one person would be on the hook every week. However, none of my team had really signed on for this kind of invasive schedule. I was there to listen to the news, and the expectation was that I was going to support the change. Our team sat politely as the new policy—and a little more of our private lives—would be surrendered. One member of our team was a young woman in her twenties, the youngest on our team. She had a habit in meetings like this of listening without really make much eye contact. But she was smart, and her questions were usually good ones. In the course of the meeting, the news of being on call 24-7 was presented. I tried not to show emotion and waited for the reaction of the rest of the team. Something then happened that was very magical. The young woman paused, broke her silence, and asked, "If we agree to take this one, will we be given the tools to support it? Like company cell phones?" This was *brilliant*. What she was choosing to do was negotiate the terms of the change. I developed new respect for her. Her argument opened my eyes to new options. She, in effect, was saying, "I will support the change if I am given x, y, and z." As you decide on supporting the change, one option is to negotiate terms of the change. This is an option that is often overlooked but is very powerful. You may wonder what happened to the young woman. She grew tired of the company quickly, as the role was not a challenge for her, and she left the company after only two years. This is a trend I tend to see with young employees—kind of a "grass is greener" mind-set. I have lost track of her, but I hope she has found happiness in her career and in her life.

STEP FOUR: DECIDE

Once you have actively heard the message of change, asked the right questions, and measured the impact of the change, you arrive at the step that is the most empowering in the process of addressing change: making a decision on supporting the change. There are many options, if we have a clear mind to see them. The most common choice is to support the change. This means buying into it and aligning your work, resources, and commitment to it. A good test to see whether you are truly committed to the change is how well you can we express your support to others. Can you explain the change and the reasons behind it to your peers, management, and customers? If not, you are not truly committed to the change.

Another option is to reject the change. In the business environment, this can be risky. You need to examine what the consequences will be if you decide to reject the change. In some extreme cases, this may mean leaving your job or being disciplined in some formal or informal manner. Despite these grim scenarios, it is imperative to understand that you do have the power to reject the change, and *no one can take that power away from you.* If you think and feel strongly that you do need to reject the change, then you need to consider whether to voice this rejection. There are no black-and-white guidelines on this. What you decide on voicing rejection depends on the culture of your organization, your relationship with management and peers, and the change itself. When in doubt, act ethically. While studying ethics during my MBA program, I heard a clear and easy definition of what is ethical: "If you don't want what you did to be a headline in the local newspaper, it is most likely unethical." If you do feel it is ethical to reject the change, consider the best time and place to do so. Voice your rejection at the time and place the change is communicated. Alternatively, voice it just to members of your department or in private, to your supervisor.

A third option that is often not considered is to accept the change with conditions. For a good example of this, refer to the story at the start of this chapter. The young woman on our team had three options: (1) "I will support the change as presented"; (2) "I will reject the change" (risky, but a valid option); or (3) "I will support the change if I get the tools." She chose to negotiate terms.

Negotiation follows the format of "If x, then y"—that is, "*If* I get the tools to make the change easier to manage, *then* I will support the change."

Below are some points to consider when making the decision to support the change:

- What is the cost of rejecting the change?
- What is the cost of supporting the change?
- Can I negotiate terms of the change?
- What is the benefit of supporting the change?
- What is the benefit of rejecting the change?
- Is it ethical to support the change as stated?
- Is it ethical to reject the change?
- Can I live with myself if I accept the change?
- Can I live with myself if I reject the change?
- If I choose to negotiate, with whom?
- If I reject the change, am I prepared to leave my job?

Although this step in addressing change can be the most challenging, as well as the most risky, it is at the same time the most powerful. To avoid being a victim, you need to realize you have the power to accept, reject, or negotiate change. And *no one can take this power from you.* As always, the most important point here is to address change *actively* and avoid being the victim of change.

Looking Ahead: Steps one through three have laid the foundation for making a decision on the change, step four. Based on due diligence and informed decision, the next action step is to follow through, step five. If you have decided to negotiate the terms of the change—timing, phases, conditions, and so forth—you will do the negotiations in step five. The follow-through is also where you touch base with your business partners to confirm their support and level of commitment to the change.

Progress: We are at step four, Decide.

Here are the nine steps of empowered change management:

1) Hear the change: Make the assumption that the message of change you hear will be important and will impact you.

2) Ask questions: If you do not fully understand the change or its potential impact, it is your job to ask questions. But make sure they are the right questions.

3) Measure the impact: What are the benefits of the change? When will they be realized? What is the measure of success for the change?

4) Decide: Decide whether you will support the change as stated or negotiate the terms of the change. This is the most empowering step of the nine!

5) Follow through: Do the follow-through(s) that are needed based on your decision.

6) Implement: Own and act on your responsibilities to implement the change. Understand how problems will be escalated during implementation.

7) Track the change: Ensure that the change is being tracked. Identify the metrics and see that they are being captured.

8) Report the success: Ensure that the right teams and decision makers are fed the correct metrics around the now-implemented change. Report any peripheral or unexpected successes to the right teams. Get sign-off that the change was successful based on agreed-upon metrics.

9) Celebrate the change: Allow the organization to enjoy the success brought about by the change. This can be a morale-building opportunity. Even if the change was not entirely successful, as long as you have engaged actively in the process, you can still find reasons to celebrate.

DECIDE—WORK SHEET:

1) What will be the risks of rejecting the change?	
2) If I reject the change, can I voice a strong argument why I am rejecting?	
3) What are the costs to my customers, my organization, my team, or myself if I reject the change?	

4) What are the risks if I support the change?	
5) What are the costs to my customer, my organization, my team, and myself if I support the change?	
6) What are the benefits to supporting the change?	

7) What are the benefits to rejecting the change?	
8) Is it ethical to reject the change?	
9) Is it ethical to support the change?	
10) Can I negotiate terms of the change?	

11) Whom can I negotiate terms with?	
12) Can I articulate the terms of the change that are important to me?	

Notes:

Chapter 6

Step Five: Follow Through

Executive Summary: The key to step number five in change management is action. You need to take action on any follow-up items that have surfaced in the previous steps. This is where you need to follow up if you have decided to negotiate terms of the change.

Background Story:

As a young man, I completed high school and gave thought to what would come next in my life journey. In my adolescence I had an interest in architecture. But as I passed through my teen years, my interests changed. I found a lot of joy in music and was in a couple of bands that had some paid gigs. Just finishing high school, I was extremely drawn to pursuing music. But at the same time, I realized that a music career, especially one based around performance, was a very tough road indeed. In short, coming out of high school, I was unsure of my next steps. After a lot of thought, I decided to take general classes in science and language at my local community college. After I enrolled and started my classes, I found that energy at the school was low. Students did not seem very engaged. To me they appeared to do the minimal amount of work to earn a B. There was a general feeling that students were there because of limited finances or insufficient grades and credentials to be accepted at prestigious universities. During the coming weeks, I discovered I did not care for math or physics. I was on the staff of the student newspaper and wrote regular articles that were published. But overall I felt lost. To paraphrase Joseph Campbell, who said, "Follow your bliss," I had not found my niche, my bliss. I felt discouraged and somewhat lost. Halfway through the semester, I was seriously thinking of dropping out. I gave this a lot of thought. I came to the conclusion that since I had already paid tuition and bought the textbooks, I might as well finish what I had started. Despite some negatives, I followed through and completed the semester. I have thanked myself many, many times for doing so. Afterward, I found a job as a machine operator at a local textile factory. I worked there for three years and saved enough money to return to college—this time at a well-known university out of state. If I had not completed the semester just out of high school—if I had not followed through—returning to college would have been much, much harder. Moreover, I might not have earned my BA, which, years later, allowed me to enter and complete an MBA program at the University of St. Thomas.

In business, as in life, follow-through is critical to success.

STEP FIVE: FOLLOW THROUGH

Once the decision has been made on the change, the next step is to follow through. In most cases this is follow-through on the decision to support the change. To successfully roll out the change, you need to understand several pieces around the change. To successfully implement it, you need to understand timing, changes in resources, relationships, responsibility, and roles.

If you have decided to negotiate terms around the change, this is when you follow through. For the most part, this will mean a discussion with your supervisor. You need to decide the best time and place to have this discussion. It might also mean negotiating with your department peers, business team, or even business partners in collaborative teams. Regardless of whom we bring in, the key to successful negotiation is to come to agreement on terms. Think of terms as, "I (we) will support _____ if I (we) get _____." When you have agreement on the terms, you have a successful negotiation. If you can't come to agreement, the best option is to consider key points in discussion to understand concerns and limitations from all sides.

If you have decided *not* to support the change under any condition, you need to confirm that management understands your position. Do not enter into this lightly. Consequences from not supporting a change that has been agreed upon by management can be severe. You leave yourself vulnerable in a number of ways if you decide not to support the change. This situation will be quite rare if you consider the option of negotiation, but it is critical to empowerment to understand that you *do* have the option of *not* supporting the change and that no one can take this power from you!

Below are some bullet points to consider for following through:

- What is the timing of the change?
- Will the change be implemented in phases?
- Will the change impact existing business relationships?
- How will implementation of the change be measured?

- Will the change impact existing roles?
- Will the change be permanent or temporary?
- Will the change impact the products or services of the organization?
- How will the implementation of the change impact our customers?

In summary, how you follow through on the change will depend on whether you want to support the change as presented, negotiate the change, or, in extreme cases, decide not to support the change under any circumstances. In the real world, this last scenario will be unusual. Still, recognition that rejection of the change is a valid option is critical to empowerment. As always, the more *active* we are in addressing the change, the less we are its victims. When in doubt, be engaged!

Looking Ahead: We have just covered step five, follow through. Looking forward, step six is implementation. In the next chapter we will consider the plan for and execution of the implementation. In step six, you will confirm that your management; business partners; and teams, both upstream and downstream, have committed to the change. You will also, confirm phases of the implementation and dates and map out where to report problems in implementation.

Progress: We are at step five, follow through.

Here are the nine steps of empowered change management:

1) Hear the change: Make the assumption that the message of change you hear will be important and will impact you.

2) Ask questions: If you do not fully understand the change or its potential impact, it is your job to ask questions. But make sure they are the right questions.

3) Measure the impact: What are the benefits of the change? When will they be realized? What is the measure of success for the change?

4) Decide: Decide whether you will support the change as stated or negotiate the terms of the change. This is the most empowering step of the nine!

5) Follow through: Do the follow-through(s) that are needed based on your decision.

6) Implement: Own and act on your responsibilities to implement the change. Understand how problems will be escalated during implementation.

7) Track the change: Ensure that the change is being tracked. Identify the metrics and see that they are being captured.

8) Report the success: Ensure that the right teams and decision makers are fed the correct metrics around the now-implemented change. Report any peripheral or unexpected successes to the right teams. Get sign-off that the change was successful based on agreed-upon metrics.

9) Celebrate the change: Allow the organization to enjoy the success brought about by the change. This can be a morale-building opportunity. Even if the change was not entirely successful, as long as you have engaged actively in the process, you can still find reasons to celebrate.

FOLLOW THROUGH—WORK SHEET:

1) What is my list of items I need to follow through on?	
2) Do I know whom I need to follow through with?	
3) Have I noted all the phases of implementation?	

4) Do I need to sign off on any follow-through? If so, from whom?	
5) Do I understand what teams and business partners will be impacted by the change?	
6) What roles will be impacted by the change?	

7) Do we have buy-in from impacted teams and business partners?	
8) Do we know if the change will be temporary or permanent?	
9) Is follow-through needed around changes in products or services?	

10) Do we need to follow through with our customers?	
Notes:	

Chapter 7

Step Six: Implementation

Executive Summary: If you have decided to support the change, in step number six, you plan for and execute implementation. In this step you confirm that your management; business partners; and teams, both upstream and downstream, have committed to the change. You confirm phases of the implementation and dates and map out where to report problems in implementation.

Background Story:

The biggest, most expensive initiative I was ever directly involved in was developing software for a state on the East Coast of the United States. The software was supposed to track records, transitions, payments, and other financials for which the state was responsible. This was not a million-dollar project. This was not tens of millions. It was *hundreds* of millions of dollars in requirements, design, coding, testing, and delivery. For whatever reason, the state did not track the project directly. Instead, they assembled a team of contractors to serve as a buffer between us and the state officials to monitor our work and report gaps and issues. Much work had been done. Code had been written and was being tested in an environment as close to real production as possible. This project had taken a couple of years of work from multiple requirements, design, and development teams. We were in the final stages and working on planning around rollout into production. Friction had developed over several months. The contractors that reported to the state were slowing the process down considerably. Time ran on, and budgets became unworkable. The sad ending is that the multimillion-dollar work was never put into production for the state. My point here is not to lay blame— although there is plenty of blame to go around. The point of this dismal and costly story is that there was no implementation of any of our work. To me this is an unforgivable waste. Ultimately the costs of not implementing were passed on to the innocent third parties—the tax payers of the state. This is an extreme example of the cost of lack of implementation.

STEP SIX: IMPLEMENTATION

If you have committed to support the change, either as presented, or by way of negotiation, you come to the next step in empowered mastery of change: implementing the change. This step may appear straightforward, and for the most part, it is. However, there are some things to consider to implement, or roll out, the change. Teams both upstream and down in the business process need to be prepared for the change. A suggestion is to reach out to your business partners who will be impacted to make sure all are on the same page with regard to buy-in and actual implementation timing.

At the individual level, do some planning to make sure you have addressed all potential gaps. This will give the change the best chance for success. Your planner or calendar can help with change implementation. If problems arise during implementation, you need to understand how, and to whom, you should report these issues and who is responsible for resolving them.

Here is a list of items that can be used as a resource in preparing to implement the change:

- Reach out to business partners both upstream and downstream to confirm they are supporting the change.
- Confirm with business partners, teammates, and your

supervisor the timing of the implementation of the change.

- Use your electronic calendar or planner to mark off and remind you of the timing of the change.
- Record additional resources and tasks driven by implementation in your calendar.
- Get or create a mapping of escalation contacts if problems around implementation arise.
- If the change may impact your daily or weekly schedule, make sure that this has been communicated to the right people. This includes your family, husband, wife, or partner!

In some ways, implementing the change is the most exciting step in empowered mastery of change, since this is where the change comes to fruition: it manifests in your life. A small effort in preparation for rollout of change will deliver big dividends in successful implementation. If you take an *active* role in implementation, you will be a better employee, teammate, business partner, or leader, and a more responsible and successful individual. If you manage yourself well in this phase, you are one step closer to being a master of change!

Looking Ahead: The step we have just covered is implementation. Looking forward we will consider what is needed to track the change. This step number seven assumes the change has been implemented. In tracking the change, we need to tie back to the original reasons that drove the change. Proper metrics, and tracking provides the data needed to assess if the change has been successful, or not, and gather measurement of the impact, the delta.

Progress: We are at step 6, implementation.

Here are the nine steps of empowered change management:

1) Hear the change: Make the assumption that the message of change you hear will be important and will impact you.

2) Ask questions: If you do not fully understand the change or its potential impact, it is your job to ask questions. But make sure they are the right questions.

3) Measure the impact: What are the benefits of the change? When will they be realized? What is the measure of success for the change?

4) Decide: Decide whether you will support the change as stated or negotiate the terms of the change. This is the most empowering

step of the nine!

5) Follow through: Do the follow-through(s) that are needed based on your decision.

6) Implement: Own and act on your responsibilities to implement the change. Understand how problems will be escalated during implementation.

7) Track the change: Ensure that the change is being tracked. Identify the metrics and see that they are being captured.

8) Report the success: Ensure that the right teams and decision makers are fed the correct metrics around the now-implemented change. Report any peripheral or unexpected successes to the right teams. Get sign-off that the change was successful based on agreed-upon metrics.

9) Celebrate the change: Allow the organization to enjoy the success brought about by the change. This can be a morale-building opportunity. Even if the change was not entirely successful, as long as you have engaged actively in the process, you can still find reasons to celebrate.

IMPLEMENTATION—WORK SHEET:

1) Have you identified the business teams upstream that will be impacted by the change?	
2) Do you have buy-in or sign-off from the teams and business partners upstream?	
3) Have you identified the business teams downstream that will be impacted by the change?	
4) Do you have buy-in or sign-off from the teams and business partners downstream?	
5) Will implementation occur in phases? If so, do you know the implementation dates for each phase?	
6) Are teams both upstream, and downstream agreed on the implementation dates?	

7) Have you plugged the milestone dates into your calendar?	
8) Have escalation teams been identified and communicated to those who will be supporting and tracking the change?	
9) Do you have contact info for the named escalation teams?	
10) Have you noted any changes in resources, processes, or tasks needed from you to support the change?	
11) Have you communicated to your business partners, peers, teams, and department potential changes in your availability?	

12) Have you communicated to your family, spouse, or life partner potential changes in your availability?	

Notes:

Chapter 8

Step Seven: Track the Change

Executive Summary:

Following implementation of the change, a best practice is to track the impact of the change. The measurement of success needs to tie back to the underlying reasons for change. These are identified in the first three steps of empowered change mastery: step one, hear the change; step two, ask questions; and, especially, step three, measure the impact of the change.

Background Story:

My mother had had multiple health issues. She turned eighty-eight last year. At that age it is rare not to have health issues and a decline in quality of life. My sisters and I, along with close friends of the family, worked to assess the best place for her to be, given her age, decline in health, and need for care. My mother had lived in a small city in Southern Wisconsin her whole life. My sister lives in Nashville along with my niece and her family, while my nephew is in Chicago with his family. And I live north of Minneapolis. When we realized that my mom would need 24-7 care, I asked her whether she wanted me to look for a care center in the Twin Cities. I knew what the answer would be before I asked the question. My mom wanted to stay in southern Wisconsin, to be close to her many friends. When she first entered a nursing home in my hometown, she was not happy. The nursing home was less than five years old and was a beautiful facility. But my mom said she could not relate to the people in her section. She complained about the food. She complained that she was not allowed to leave the facility unattended. But over many visits and many conversations, she began to see that this was probably the best place for her to be. Despite her complaints, she formed friendships and got to know all her fellow residents by first name.

In the last couple months another health issue arose. My mom began to have difficulty breathing. After some diagnostics, her doctors realized that there was fluid building up in her lungs that had to be removed. They also discovered a possibly cancerous tumor on her left lung. After having the fluid removed, my mom felt better for a few weeks. But soon, more fluid built up and had to be drained once again. The procedure was painful and had to be prematurely. My mom was left in this kind of limbo but returned to her nursing home. Shortly thereafter, I received a phone call from my sister that mom had fallen while reaching for something on the floor and was back in the hospital for x-rays and rest. Her vital functions were monitored. Within a day or two, my mom's condition worsened. She became less and less responsive. She could not speak, only nod her head "yes" or shake it "no." Because of the tracking—the health monitoring—at the hospital, it was clear that my mom's kidneys were failing. This information was passed on to my sister and me. We knew this was a serious situation and were prepared emotionally for what was to come. The following morning, I received a call from my sister that my mother had passed away very early that morning.

The above is an extreme example of the importance of tracking. Although my mom had last entered the hospital because of a fall, the hospital's tracking her vital signs provided critical information about her rapidly declining health, information that helped the family prepare.

STEP SEVEN: TRACK THE CHANGE

Potential reasons for the change may include: a better, more efficient process; compliance with external requirements, such as new federal, state, or local regulations; development of a better or newer product or service; to reduce costs and/or increase profits. The most important reasons tie directly to the customer. Among these are faster speed to market, increased quality in product or services, and better customer service.

If the reason for the change was to increase efficiency, you could track its impact (its success) by measuring resource hours—both before and after—to calculate actual savings. If the change was in response to regulations, you may need to bring in business partners and potentially a legal team to ensure compliance. As a member of a systems development team for a nationally known bank, I would estimate that about 80 percent of my work as a liaison between senior business partners and development teams was directly related to new federal regulations. To quantify speed-to-market delta (delta is used in business to refer to the impact, or change from the previous state), compare before and after change numbers. Measurement of success of a new product or service will take longer to track. Depending on the particular product or new service, it may take a year or more to collect data to compare with projected revenue and profit models.

I do need to mention that, in some organizations, there may be no formal procedure for tracking the impact of the change. If this is the case in your organization, you have an opportunity to bring value by creating a process. Proceed cautiously here. Diplomatically raise the question to leadership, and make sure you have full buy-in from your supervisor, management, and all key stakeholders before committing to building, or helping to build, this process.

Below are some things to consider when tracking the change:

- Does tracking the change tie back to the original underlying reason(s) for the change?
- Are there secondary benefits that were not part of the original justification?
- If the change was driven by compliance, is there sign-off by your business partners that compliance has been met?
- Are the benefits of the change perceived to be internal (e.g., lower costs, increase profits)?
- Are the benefits of the change perceived to be external (e.g., better quality product, services)?

- Is measurement of success to be found in resource hours?
- How can customer-related impact be measured (e.g., increased satisfaction, larger client base)?

In summary, if a change has been implemented, best practice is to track the success of the change. The measure of success should primarily tie back to the original reason(s) for the change. If no formal process is in place, you have an opportunity to help build one to track success. This opportunity should be approached diplomatically, with buy-in and support, starting with your supervisor and management. If you have good metrics and tools in place to track success, you are well on the way to being an empowered master of change.

Looking Ahead: We have just covered step seven which is to track the change. The next step, step eight is reporting of the change. Capturing proper tracking data, with appropriate metrics is the foundation for step eight, reporting on the success of the change. The key to step eight is communications. Proper reporting of the change will make meaningful the impact of the change to those who need to know of it, and in a way that is easy to consume.

Progress: We are at step seven, track the change.

Here are the nine steps of empowered change management:

1) Hear the change: Make the assumption that the message of change you hear will be important and will impact you.

2) Ask questions: If you do not fully understand the change or its potential impact, it is your job to ask questions. But make sure they are the right questions.

3) Measure the impact: What are the benefits of the change? When will they be realized? What is the measure of success for the change?

4) Decide: Decide whether you will support the change as stated or negotiate the terms of the change. This is the most empowering step of the nine!

5) Follow through: Do the follow-through(s) that are needed based on your decision.

6) Implement: Own and act on your responsibilities to implement the change. Understand how problems will be escalated during implementation.

7) Track the change: Ensure that the change is being tracked. Identify the metrics and see that they are being captured.

8) Report the success: Ensure that the right teams and decision makers are fed the correct metrics around the now-implemented change. Report any peripheral or unexpected successes to the right teams. Get sign-off that the change was successful based on agreed-upon metrics.

9) Celebrate the change: Allow the organization to enjoy the success brought about by the change. This can be a morale-building opportunity. Even if the change was not entirely successful, as long as you have engaged actively in the process, you can still find reasons to celebrate.

TRACK THE CHANGE—WORK SHEET:

1) Will the tracking metrics tie back to the root reasons that drove the change?	
2) Will analytics be able to track secondary benefits delivered by the change?	
3) If the change is to address compliance or external regulations, will the tracking satisfy the requirements?	

4) If the change was around compliance or regulatory issues, what group provides sign-off that the change meets compliance?	
5) Have the metrics to be used been agreed upon by management, and all stakeholders?	
6) Will the metrics used quantify the benefits and costs?	

7) Will the benefits, and costs of the change be trackable in resource hours? Contractor hours? System processing time, or system resources?	
8) What metrics will be used to track customer impact from the change?	
9) What metrics will be used to measure customer satisfaction?	

10) Will tracking data be collected daily? Weekly? Monthly? Quarterly?	
Notes:	

Chapter 9

Step Eight: Report the Success

Executive Summary:

Tracking the impact of the change has little value until it is reported to the right people. Ideally, you are reporting the success of the change. Reports of success need to tie back to the reasons for the change. For example, if the goal of the change was to reduce costs, then reporting needs to show how costs were reduced in ways and metrics that are meaningful. If the change was introduced to increase customer satisfaction, the reporting needs to capture how customer satisfaction has increased. In addition, if peripheral positive or negative impacts resulted from the change, these need to be reported as well to the right people in ways that are understandable and meaningful.

Background Story:

If you have attended business school or have worked with reviewing or preparing company financial reports, you will be familiar with income statements, which are also sometimes known as the "profit and loss statement" or "statement of revenue and expense." These statements track all sales, fees, and revenue and all costs or expenses the company (or organization) has incurred during a specific period of accounting time. Those that receive the most attention are income statements over a company's (or organization's) previous fiscal year. These are customarily published in summary format in a company's annual report. But they are also usually produced on a monthly and quarterly basis. These statements show the profit or loss for a company over a period of time. Since these statements show actual profit, they are critical for people tracking the success of the company, such as management, business partners, and investors. In a broad sense, these income statements are formalized tracking reports. They report changes in sales, revenue, and fees, as well as all costs the company has incurred. In a very real way, they are reporting success in sales, contracts, and so forth when weighed against costs to produce the company's products and services. However, a report of success needs to tie back to the original reasons that drove the need for the change. It should be in a form and use metrics that are meaningful to the owners, managers, and stakeholders of the change. To give a few examples, if the reason for the change was to meet a regulatory requirement, such as compliance, then the report needs to capture the success of meeting compliance. If the change was introduced to reduce expenses, then the report needs to state the level of success delivered in resource time, contractor time, raw-materials savings, or lowered management and administrative costs. If the change was introduced to improve product design, the report needs to refer to greater customer satisfaction, increased durability, end-user satisfaction, or other meaningful measures of product improvement. When success of the change is reported, it becomes real to those who requested the change, those who worked to support it, and all those who benefited from it, including clients or customers.

STEP EIGHT: REPORT THE SUCCESS

In the previous step, we used appropriate metrics to track the change. These metrics need to tie back to the original goals projected for the change and also identify any additional benefits it provided. Once you have enough valid information from tracking the change, your next step is to report on its success. The key point in this step is communication. Depending on the organization, the formal process of reporting on success of the change may fall to a specific team or department. If you do not know which team holds this accountability, it is your job to find out. It is best practice to check within your team or department. This is an important step in the change process. It closes the loop from the reasons for the change, implementation of the change, tracking and communicating success to the right stakeholders, and delivery of this message to the right people, ordinarily those who argued for the change, often middle or upper management. Below is a checklist to consider when you arrive at step eight, report the success of the change:

- Has the tracking history been long enough that you are highly confident in reporting on the change?
- Has the department or team who should receive the report been identified?
- If the team to receive the report has not been identified, who can do so?
- Will the reporting metrics close the loop and tie back to the original reasons for the change?
- Is reporting closed-ended (one and done), or will it be ongoing?
- If the reporting is ongoing, what is the frequency of the reporting—daily, weekly, monthly, quarterly, etc.?
- If the report indicates the change has not met its objectives, who owns the gap?

- What person or team decides whether the change has been successful?

- Has the proper person or team signed off that either the change is successful or that it has not met the projected goals and needs additional work?

- If your team is to provide help on reporting, have standard metrics been agreed upon?

Not all teams have input or ownership in step number eight, but it is a critical step for the benefit of the organization or company. By reporting back with appropriate metrics, based on a reasonable tracking history, the loop will be closed between justification for the change and the actual output of the implemented change. The measure of success of the change is reported back to the right people, including key stakeholders and business owners. In this step, the very real impact of the change is communicated back to the decision makers so that a determination of success can be made. When you regard this step as part of your overall process and complete it with diligence, you will see that you have used best practices and have become a master of the management of change. Only one more step remains in the process of becoming an empowered master of change.

Looking Ahead: We have just finished step eight, report the change. Optimistically, this means reporting the success of the change. We made decisions about what metrics to use, the form of the reporting, and considered the teams we needed to provide reporting to. If we have any measure of success, or at best if it has been a learning experience we come to step nine, celebrate the success of the change. We can use the success of the change, or other outcomes of the change to build relationships. This can be relationships within our departments, or teams, or with our business partners. We can even celebrate the change in a way that builds our organizational culture. The cycle is complete as we finish step nine, celebrate the success.

Progress: We are at step eight, report the change.

Here are the nine steps of empowered change management:

1) Hear the change: Make the assumption that the message of change you hear will be important and will impact you.

2) Ask questions: If you do not fully understand the change or its potential impact, it is your job to ask questions. But make sure they are the right questions.

3) Measure the impact: What are the benefits of the change? When will they be realized? What is the measure of success for the change?

4) Decide: Decide whether you will support the change as stated or negotiate the terms of the change. This is the most empowering step of the nine!

5) Follow through: Do the follow-through(s) that are needed based on your decision.

6) Implement: Own and act on your responsibilities to implement the change. Understand how problems will be escalated during implementation.

7) Track the change: Ensure that the change is being tracked. Identify the metrics and see that they are being captured.

8) Report the success: Ensure that the right teams and decision makers are fed the correct metrics around the now-implemented change. Report any peripheral or unexpected successes to the right teams. Get sign-off that the change was successful based on agreed-upon metrics.

9) Celebrate the change: Allow the organization to enjoy the success brought about by the change. This can be a morale-building opportunity. Even if the change was not entirely successful, as long as you have engaged actively in the process, you can still find reasons to celebrate.

REPORT THE SUCCESS—WORK SHEET:

1) How much tracking data do you have?	
2) When did you start tracking data?	
3) What is your level of confidence based the current volume of tracking history?	

4) What teams are to receive tracking data?	
5) If the teams to receive tracking data are not defined, who can define them?	
6) Will the tracking data collected tie back to the agreed-upon metrics?	

7) Will the reporting be "one and done" or ongoing?	
8) If reporting is ongoing, what is the frequency of reporting?	
9) Can the data be used to validate the success of the change?	

10) Who validates the tracking data?	
11) If the data indicates the change was not successful or only partly successful, who needs to be notified?	
12) Does the data require sign-off? Who signs off?	

13) What team uses the data to validate the change?	
14) Who makes the decision on whether the change has been successful?	
15) If the tracking data is to be supplied to other teams, does the reporting meet agreed-upon standards?	

Notes:

Chapter 10

Step Nine: Celebrate the Change

Executive Summary:

Celebrating the change is the final step in the nine-step system of empowered change management. If the change has been articulated clearly, planned for well, implemented carefully, tracked diligently, and reported in metrics that are meaningful, the chances for a successful change are assured. In taking the final step of celebrating the change, you have an opportunity to strengthen business relationships and build stronger teams and a more durable organizational culture.

Background Story:

Marriage is one of the biggest life-changing events, on the same level as births and deaths. For those of us who have been married, the marriage ceremony is will always be in our memories. Even if details of the honeymoon may fade, the ceremony itself will remain a vivid memory. We will usually remember where the ceremony was, the day of the week, and who attended. We will also recall who presided—even if we do not remember the name of the priest, rabbi, or judge. At its core marriage is celebration of a change. It is a public celebration of the union of two people who have committed to support, tend to, partner with, and love each other. It is a joyous celebration that announces not only the bonding of two people to each other but also that of each mate to a new family. Marriage is a huge life change, and the marriage ceremony is a celebration of this change.

In the business or organizational environment, the success of a change that has been agreed upon and delivered can also celebrated. Celebration encourages bonding within teams, between teams, and throughout the organization.

Step nine, the final step in management of business change, is the icing on the cake, the bow on the package. And yet I have rarely witnessed it firsthand. In fairness, I could have called this step "mourn the change." But it is best to stay optimistic, especially in the business world, and for this reason, I would rather refer to it as "celebrate" the change.

STEP NINE: CELEBRATE THE CHANGE

Success lends itself to celebration. The fruits of a successful change may be announced at an all-hands meeting, a department meeting, or a team meeting or noted in corporate or even public communications, such as trade journals, magazines, or newspapers. Achieving success in business is most often a difficult process. A celebration of success will energize the entire organization, regardless of whether everyone was involved in the change. This is the time for feeling great satisfaction that the effort, the problems, the misses, and the extra hours were worth it. This can be a small moment that builds pride and company culture in a big way.

You can ask the hard question, "Are there things to celebrate if the change itself fails or is only marginally successful?" If you spend a little time reviewing the nine-step process, you will see that there certainly are things to celebrate. Starting with the first step, you have become a better listener through following the process. You are also more engaged in the change, as you ask questions and understand what drives it. You have built better relationships within your team and your organization, as you worked the steps that emphasized communication with members of your department, your team, your business partners, and even your customers. You have become a better leader through buying into the change or, conversely, presenting strong reasons to push back against it. You have become a better follower by committing to support the change. This includes reporting to the right decision makers regarding any gaps or problems as the change was being implemented and metrics were collected. You have become a better employee through gaining a better understanding of what was driving the change and making the extra effort to look for accountability. Finally, you have become more empowered as an individual, no longer a victim of the change. The key to being empowered is to be active and engaged in the process.

Progress: We are at step nine, celebrate the change. We have completed the cycle of empowered change management.

Here are the nine steps of empowered change management:

1) Hear the change: Make the assumption that the message of change you hear will be important and will impact you.

2) Ask questions: If you do not fully understand the change or its potential impact, it is your job to ask questions. But make sure they are the right questions.

3) Measure the impact: What are the benefits of the change? When

will they be realized? What is the measure of success for the change?

4) Decide: Decide whether you will support the change as stated or negotiate the terms of the change. This is the most empowering step of the nine!

5) Follow through: Do the follow-through(s) that are needed based on your decision.

6) Implement: Own and act on your responsibilities to implement the change. Understand how problems will be escalated during implementation.

7) Track the change: Ensure that the change is being tracked. Identify the metrics and see that they are being captured.

8) Report the success: Ensure that the right teams and decision makers are fed the correct metrics around the now-implemented change. Report any peripheral or unexpected successes to the right teams. Get sign-off that the change was successful based on agreed-upon metrics.

9) Celebrate the change: Allow the organization to enjoy the

success brought about by the change. This can be a morale-building opportunity. Even if the change was not entirely successful, as long as you have engaged actively in the process, you can still find reasons to celebrate.

CELEBRATE THE CHANGE—WORK SHEET:

1) Did you celebrate the change at a department or team meeting?	
2) Can you add a mention of the change success to a department or team agenda?	

3) Has your boss or management sent you a thank-you about the successful change?	
4) How can you celebrate the change with others who supported the change?	
5) What benefits were delivered to your customers because of the change?	

6) Were awards given out for support of the change?	
7) Was there group recognition given for success of the change?	
8) Were customers told about the success of the change?	

9) Have the company corporate communications mentioned the success of the change in internal newsletters or press releases?	

CONLUSION

In summary, when you make the extra effort and exercise due diligence around change, the organization has a more successful change implementation, with better buy-in, reduced costs, and increased profits. Or in the case of a nonprofit, the organization becomes more efficient and provides better services at lower costs to more clients. At a personal level, you realize that you need not be a victim of change. Your best course during the change process is to remain actively engaged. By doing this, you are no longer a victim. You are instead a better worker, leader, or decision maker. You have become an empowered master of change.

GLOSSARY

Corporation	A for profit business unit that has completed articles of incorporation. Corporations are owned by their shareholders.
Delta	A business term that is used to discuss what has changed from the previous condition, or sate.
Empower	Empower is to give an individual, or a group, authority, and/or power to make decisions on things that impact their lives.
Loss	Loss is the negative balance that remains after all costs have been subtracted from all sales, and revenue for a given period of time. This can be monthly, quarterly, or annually.
Organization	A body that may be for profit, or may be non-profit, or may be not-for-profit.
Profit	Profit is the positive balance that remains after costs have been subtracted from all sales, and revenue. This can be monthly, quarterly, or annually.

BRIAN KAIL MBA

CHANGE MANAGEMENT GUIDE

ABOUT THE AUTHOR

Brian Kail, MBA, CPC, CCC is a Career and Business Coach. Brian earned an MBA at the University of St. Thomas. He holds a BA in Communications from the University of Wisconsin, Madison. Brian owns and manages Ascender Professional Coaching, LLC. (AscendProCoach.com on the web.) Brian has over thirty years' business experience holding Corporate positions in several Fortune 500 companies, including EcoLab, Piper Jaffray, SuperValu, and US Bank. In addition to his work in career, and business, Brian is a student of comparative religions. A lover of language, in addition to his native English, Brian speaks German fluently, and is in the process of learning Egyptian Coptic.

Brian's next book will be on the topic of career development.